NIMITZ AIRCRAFT CARRIER

BY QUINN M. ARNOLD

CREATIVE EDUCATION • CREATIVE PAPERBACKS

Published by Creative Education and Creative Paperbacks
P.O. Box 227, Mankato, Minnesota 56002
Creative Education and Creative Paperbacks are imprints
of The Creative Company
www.thecreativecompany.us

Design by The Design Lab
Production by Chelsey Luther
Art direction by Rita Marshall
Printed in the United States of America

Photographs by Corbis (HUGH GENTRY/Reuters, Stocktrek
Images/Stocktrek Images), Flickr (United States Navy), Getty
Images (Giovanni Colla/Stocktrek Images)

Library of Congress Cataloging-in-Publication Data
Arnold, Quinn M.
Nimitz aircraft carrier / by Quinn M. Arnold.
p. cm. — (Now that's big!)
Includes bibliographical references and index.
Summary: A high-interest introduction to the size, speed, and pur-
pose of one of the world's largest aircraft carriers, including a brief
history and what the future holds for the Nimitz aircraft carrier.

ISBN 978-1-60818-712-6 (hardcover)
ISBN 978-1-62832-308-5 (pbk)
ISBN 978-1-56660-748-3 (eBook)
1. Nimitz (Ship: CVN-68)—Juvenile literature. 2. Aircraft
carriers—United States—Juvenile literature. 3. Nimitz Class
(Aircraft carriers)—Juvenile literature.

V874.3.A76 2016
359.9/48350973—dc23   2015045208

CCSS: RI.1.1, 2, 3, 4, 5, 6, 7; RI.2.1, 2, 4, 5, 6, 7, 10; RF.1.1, 3, 4;
RF.2.3, 4

First Edition HC 9 8 7 6 5 4 3 2 1
First Edition PBK 9 8 7 6 5 4 3 2 1

TABLE OF CONTENTS

What ship is so big that it has its own hospital? The USS *Nimitz* is more than 23 stories tall. It is one of the biggest aircraft carriers in the world.

Catapults help launch airplanes off the ship's flight deck.

Nimitz is 1,092 feet (333 m) long. It is 252 feet (76.8 m) wide. The flight deck is flat. Military aircraft take off and land there. An airplane can take off every 20 seconds!

The USS *Nimitz* is 1 of 10 *Nimitz* class ships. They were made for the United States Navy between 1968 and 2006. *Nimitz* ships run on nuclear energy. They need to be refueled only once every 20 years!

Forty basketball courts could fit on the flight deck.

Four propellers help the ship move. They are 21 feet (6.4 m) tall. Behind the propellers are two rudders. The rudders turn the ship. Each is 29 feet (8.8 m) tall and 22 feet (6.7 m) long.

Special crews prepare the flight deck for takeoffs and landings.

Nimitz ships can go more than 34.5 miles (55.5 km) per hour. They can store a lot of food and supplies. Up to 6,000 people work on each big ship.

Five or more naval ships form a carrier strike group.

Aircraft carriers are important to the U.S. Navy. Most carry 60 to 80 aircraft. Sometimes they travel in groups with other warships. They are always ready for battle.

Large elevators lift aircraft to the flight deck from the hangar below.

The ships also help after natural disasters. They can carry more than 110 tons (100 t) of supplies. Helicopters fly from the ships to rescue people.

Like the Nimitz *carriers,* Ford *ships are built in Newport News, Virginia.*

Ford class carriers will take over for *Nimitz* one day. Until then, *Nimitz* ships will continue to carry military aircraft for the U.S. Navy.

HOW BIG

ANACONDA
◂····· *25 ft (7.6 m)* ·····▸

SEMITRAILER TRUCK
◂····· *70 ft (21.3 m)* ·····▸

BLUE WHALE
◂····· *100 ft (30.5 m)* ·····▸

BOEING 737 MAX 8
◂····· *138.2 ft (42.1 m)* ·····▸

NIMITZ AIRCRAFT CARRIER
◂·············· *1,092 ft (333 m)* ··············▸

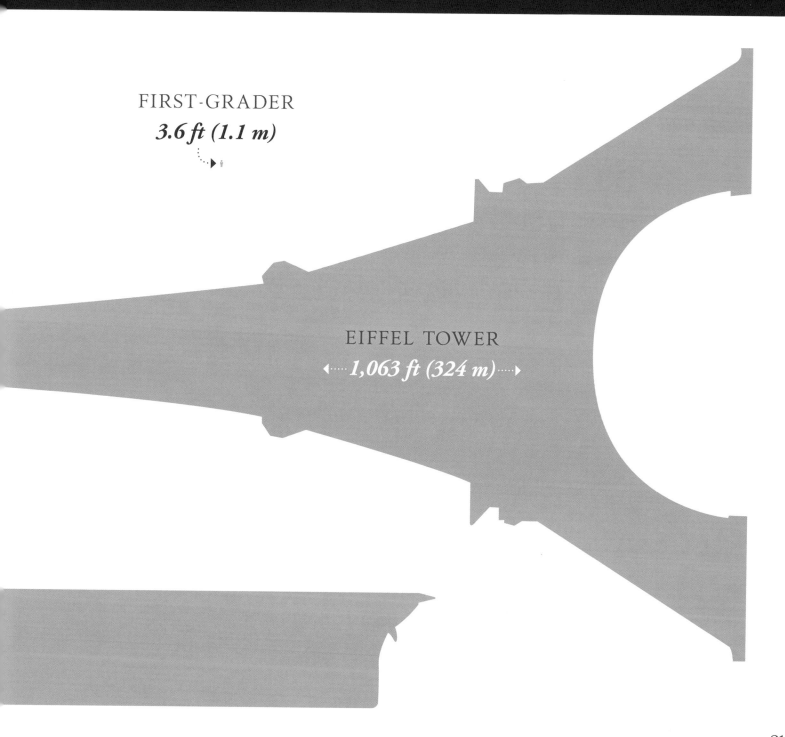

FIRST-GRADER
3.6 ft (1.1 m)

EIFFEL TOWER
◄····1,063 ft (324 m)····►

GLOSSARY

aircraft carriers—*navy ships made to carry and launch military airplanes and helicopters*

class—*a group of similarly made ships*

flight deck—*the top level of an aircraft carrier, where planes take off and land*

natural disasters—*events such as earthquakes or storms that cause damage*

nuclear energy—*energy created from particles breaking down*

propellers—*parts powered by engines that help a ship go forward*

READ MORE

Riggs, Kate. *Battleships.*
Mankato, Minn.: Creative Education, 2016.

Von Finn, Denny. *Nimitz Aircraft Carriers.*
Minneapolis: Bellwether Media, 2013.

WEBSITES

Aircraft Carriers
http://www.navy.com/about/equipment/vessels/carriers.html
Visit the official site of the U.S. Navy to learn more about *Nimitz* and *Ford* class carriers.

All About Sink and Float
http://easyscienceforkids.com/all-about-sink-and-float/
Discover how things float. Includes a video and examples.

Note: Every effort has been made to ensure that the websites listed above are suitable for children, that they have educational value, and that they contain no inappropriate material. However, because of the nature of the Internet, it is impossible to guarantee that these sites will remain active indefinitely or that their contents will not be altered.